Weathering and Erosion

Torrey Maloof

Consultants

Sally Creel, Ed.D.
Curriculum Consultant

Leann Iacuone, M.A.T., NBCT, ATC
Riverside Unified School District

Image Credits: p.23 (top) Morley Read/Alamy; p.32 iStock; p.20 (left & right) Charles D. Winters/Science Source; p.24 (left) Georg Gerster/Science Source; p.12 (top) Louise Murray/Science Source; pp.28–29 (illustrations) J.J. Rudisill; all other images from Shutterstock.

Library of Congress Cataloging-in-Publication Data

Maloof, Torrey, author.
Weathering and erosion / Torrey Maloof.
pages cm
Summary: "Earth is constantly changing. Wind, water, and even humans change Earth's surface. The land is broken down and worn away by erosion. The Grand Canyon was made from erosion. Many other landforms were made this way, too."— Provided by publisher.
Audience: K to grade 3.
Includes index.
ISBN 978-1-4807-4611-4 (pbk.)
ISBN 978-1-4807-5078-4 (ebook)
1. Weathering—Juvenile literature.
2. Erosion—Juvenile literature.
3. Landforms—Juvenile literature. I. Title.
QE570.M35 2015
551.3'52—dc23

2014014120

Teacher Created Materials
5301 Oceanus Drive
Huntington Beach, CA 92649-1030
http://www.tcmpub.com

ISBN 978-1-4807-4611-4

Printed by: 51497
Printed in: Taiwan

Table of Contents

Ever-Changing Earth

The shape and look of Earth's surface changes over time. It never stops changing. Rivers bend. Shorelines wear away. **Valleys** grow deeper. **Canyons** grow wider. Mountains break down.

These changes can be caused by the blowing wind. Or they can be the result of running water. Ice can cause these changes, too. So can the sun's rays. Even people play a part. Earth's surface has changed a lot over the years and continues to do so!

Monument Valley in Colorado

Seven Sisters cliffs in England

Wind, Water, and More

Imagine a fierce storm. Rain pours. Winds blow wildly. What do you think the rain and wind do to Earth's surface? They change it! The wind can loosen small bits of dirt and dust. Drip by drip, the rain can wear down a mountain. This process is called **weathering**.

snowstorm

A tornado is a rotating cloud that has winds that reach up to 300 miles per hour.

Over time, wind and rain wear down Earth's surface. They break it into small pieces. These pieces are called **sediment**. Wind and water then move the sediment. They carry it away. This movement is a process known as **erosion**. Weathering and erosion can happen at the same time. They work together to change Earth's surface.

Weathering and erosion are changing this mountainside.

Small rocks, such as these, are easily carried away by this river.

Wild Waters

Sediment can blow into streams and rivers. It moves with the water on its way to the ocean. It carves into hills. It cuts into mountains. This is how valleys are made.

It is also how canyons are made. The Grand Canyon was made this way. The Grand Canyon is huge! It is 446 km (277 mi) long. And it is 2.6 km (1.6 mi) deep. A river carved the massive canyon. It took millions of years.

Where Is It?

The Colorado River runs through the Grand Canyon. But the canyon is in Arizona.

This rock shattered as ice froze in its cracks.

Freezing Ice

Sometimes, water turns to ice. This can cause weathering, too. Water can run into cracks in rocks. If the air is cold enough, the water will freeze. It turns to ice and expands, or gets bigger. When this happens, the ice widens the cracks. It can even split rocks.

Later, if the air gets warmer, the ice will melt. It will turn back into water. When this happens, erosion begins. The water carries away tiny pieces of the rock.

As ice melts, the water washes away the cracked bits of rock.

A glacier is a very large sheet of ice and snow. It moves slowly down a slope. As it moves, it cuts into nearby rocks. Over time, the glacier melts. The water carves out large valleys.

One such valley is called *Yosemite* (yoh-SEM-i-tee) *Valley*. A very long time ago, there were glaciers in Yosemite. These glaciers helped make a beautiful place to visit.

Sunny California

It is hard to imagine sunny California covered in ice. But millions of years ago, it was!

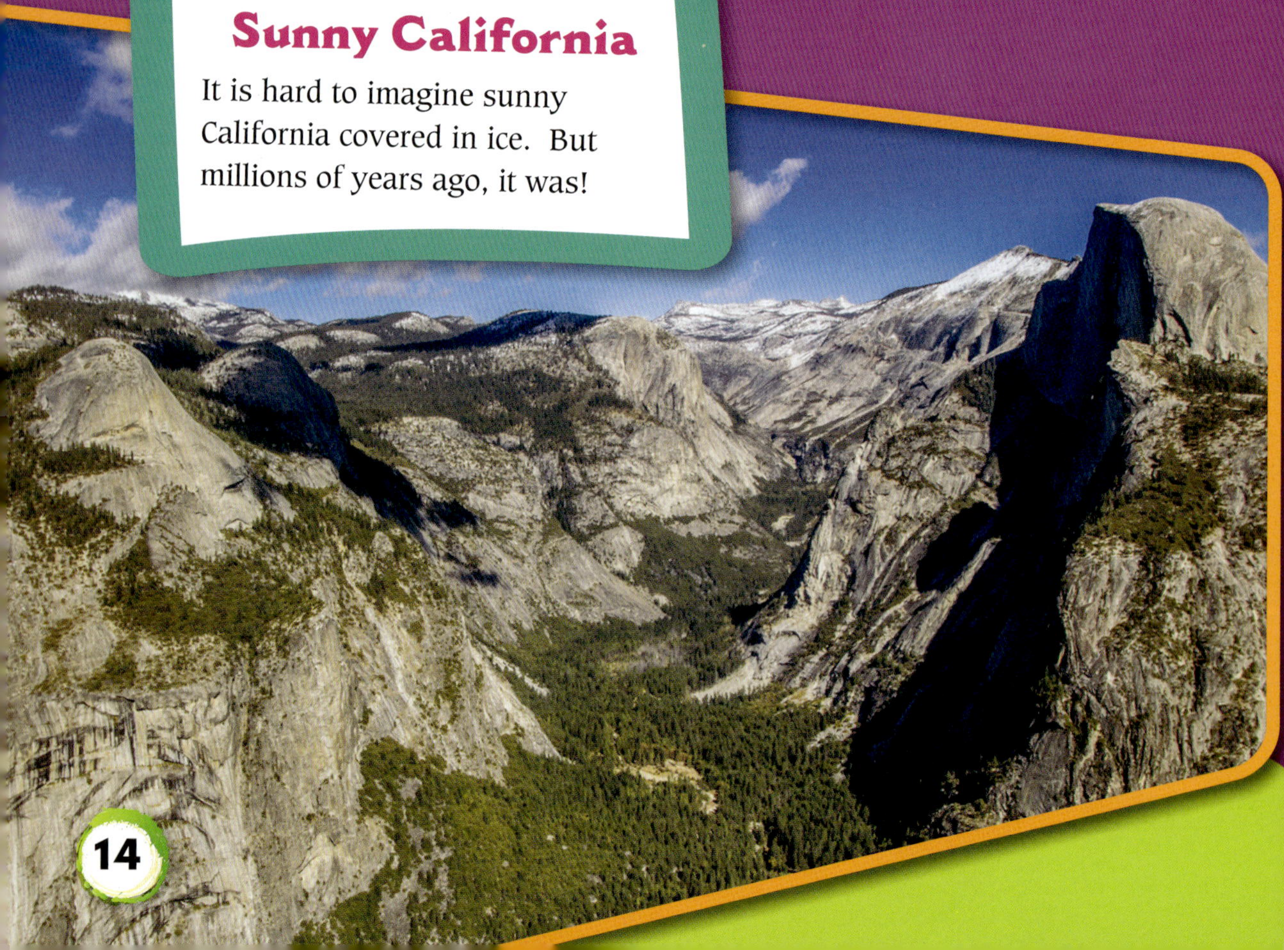

Yosemite Valley might have been carved by a glacier like this one.

Scorching Sun

The sun can change Earth's surface as well. The sun heats up rocks. Heat makes the rocks expand. Then, as the air cools, the rocks contract. They shrink.

When this happens over and over again, the rocks get very weak. After a while, they begin to crack. They eventually break apart into tiny pieces. Then, the erosion process begins and carries away the pieces of rock.

The sun's heat causes large cracks in some rocks.

Many years ago, water carried pieces of rock away to help form this canyon.

Plants and Animals

Plants and animals also cause weathering. Sometimes, soil builds up in the cracks of a rock. A seed may find its way into that soil. Then, a plant will grow in the middle of the rock! As it grows, the plant's roots crack and break apart the rock.

Animals can break apart rocks, too. Some live underground. They break apart rocks as they move through the dirt. Others break rocks above ground. They crush them by running or walking on them.

This plant will slowly break apart the rock as it grows.

Groundhogs burrow, or dig, underground. They can move over 700 pounds of dirt when digging a den.

Harsh Chemicals

Chemicals (KEM-i-kuhlz) also wear away Earth's surface. There are gases, such as oxygen, in the air and soil. New chemicals can form when these gases mix with water.

Acid is one of these chemicals. It can dissolve rocks. This means it turns the rocks to liquid. Limestone is a type of rock that acid can dissolve quickly. It can make huge cracks in the rock, too. It can even make caves and **sinkholes**!

Acid dissolves limestone.

Cool Caves

There are more than 110 caves in Carlsbad Caverns. These caves are in New Mexico. You can walk through them.

Factories pollute the air.

People Play a Part

People do not cause weathering. But they do speed it up! One way they do this is by **polluting** the air. Cars release unsafe gases. So do factories. These gases make **acid rain**. Acid rain eats away at Earth's surface.

Landslides

When plants and trees are removed, rocks and soil can suddenly slide down a hill. This is called a *landslide*.

People speed up erosion, too. One way they do this is by cutting down forests. The roots of trees help hold soil in place. When trees are cut down, the soil washes and blows away faster.

People can also stop erosion. This is known as *erosion control*. One way to do this is to build structures that hold soil and rocks in place. **Gabions** (GEY-bee-uhnz) are made of wire. They are filled with rocks. They can be used to hold dirt in place.

Another way to prevent erosion is to plant trees and plants along shorelines. The roots of these plants help keep soil in place. And they help protect the shoreline from big waves and storms.

These fields have been planted in a way that keeps the soil in place and makes a fancy pattern.

The roots of this plant will help hold the soil in place.

These gabions help hold the dirt in place.

Seeing Is Believing

It may be wind or water. It may be ice or sun. It may even be chemicals or plants. Whatever it may be, these forces create amazing sights! Weathering and erosion have made some of the most scenic places in the world. There are creepy caves. There are wonderful waterfalls. You can see crazy cliffs. Or walk through astounding arches. But hurry! These places won't last forever!

Over time, the water has eroded the cliff to make this arch.

This waterfall erodes the land around it.

Let's Do Science!

What happens when land erodes? See for yourself!

What to Get

- cardboard
- dirt
- drinking straw, cut in half
- foam cup
- modeling clay
- sharp pencil
- water

What to Do

1. Use the pencil to make a hole in the side of the cup near the bottom. Place the straw in the hole. Use the modeling clay to seal the hole.

2. Place the cardboard on the ground. Raise one end of the cardboard by placing dirt under the edge. Cover the cardboard with a thin layer of dirt.

3. Place your finger over the end of the straw and fill the cup with water.

4. Hold the cup over the raised end of the cardboard. Then, remove your finger. What happened to the dirt?

Glossary

acid rain—rain that contains dangerous chemicals caused by smoke from factories, power plants, and cars

canyons—flat areas surrounded by mountains with steep sides

chemicals—substances made from a chemical process

erosion—movement of weathered rock and sediment

gabions—wire structures filled with dirt and rocks

polluting—making dirty and unsafe

sediment—very small pieces of rock, such as sand, gravel, and dust

sinkholes—holes in the ground that are formed when soil and rocks are removed by flowing water

valleys—areas of low land between hills or mountains

weathering—the slow breakdown of rock and sediment

Index

Your Turn!

On the Hunt

The effects of weathering and erosion can be seen in many places. You might see cracks in rocks or even valleys carved by water. Go on a weathering and erosion hunt on your playground. Look for signs that wind, water, plants, or animals have changed the land.